IMAGES
of America

MOUNT HOOD
NATIONAL FOREST

Timberline Lodge was built by Works Progress Administration workers and dedicated by Pres. Franklin D. Roosevelt in 1937. It is a tourist destination, a ski resort, a hotel, and somewhere to dine, as well as a place to enjoy the fine craftsmanship and beautiful artwork that went into creating the lodge. (Courtesy of the US Forest Service.)

ON THE COVER: With the completion of the Mount Hood Loop Highway in the 1920s, mountain access became easier, and formal ski areas started to be developed. The Advertising Club Winter Sports Area (now known as Summit Ski Area) opened in December 1927. It had a wooden ski jump, toboggan slide, ski slopes, and a building that housed a lunch counter and rental shop. People could congregate and warm up at an outdoor fireplace. The skiers in this photograph are across the highway at the ski area now known as Mount Hood Skibowl. (Courtesy of the US Forest Service.)

IMAGES
of America

MOUNT HOOD
NATIONAL FOREST

Cheryl Hill

ARCADIA
PUBLISHING

Published by Arcadia Publishing
Charleston, South Carolina

Printed in the United States of America

Library of Congress Control Number: 2013945500

For all general information, please contact Arcadia Publishing:
Telephone 843-853-2070
Fax 843-853-0044
E-mail sales@arcadiapublishing.com
For customer service and orders:
Toll-Free 1-888-313-2665

Visit us on the Internet at www.arcadiapublishing.com

This book is dedicated to my wonderful partner Greg, whose companionship makes my forest explorations all the more fun.

CONTENTS

ACKNOWLEDGMENTS

Thanks go to Alexandra Wenzl, Lloyd Musser, Douglas Woycechowsky, and Tom Kloster for their help as I worked on this book. Thanks also go to Donna Henderson, Randall Henderson, Matt Carmichael, and Sara Petrocine.

Unless otherwise noted, all the images in this book appear courtesy of the US Forest Service (USFS). Other images appear courtesy of the Oregon Historical Society (OHS), the Mount Hood Cultural Center and Museum (MHCCM), the History Museum of Hood River County (HMHRC), George M. Henderson, the Columbia River Maritime Museum (CRMM), the Crag Rats (CR), the Portland Water Bureau (PWB), and the author's personal collection.

INTRODUCTION

At 11,239 feet, Mount Hood is Oregon's tallest peak and the fourth-tallest peak in the Cascade Range, which stretches from southern British Columbia, Canada, to northern California. Mount Hood is a dormant volcano and is home to 12 glaciers.

The Klickitat, the Chinook, and other Native American tribes lived in the area for hundreds of years before the arrival of white settlers. The Native Americans relied on the mighty Columbia River for fishing and transportation, and they used the forest for hunting and picking berries. They used western red cedar trees to build longhouses and canoes, and they used the cedar bark for baskets. They also utilized controlled burning to improve hunting and grazing areas.

The Native Americans had several legends about the mountain that would one day be named Mount Hood—one legend tells of two sons of the Great Spirit Sahale who both fell in love with a beautiful maiden named Loowit. She could not decide between them, so Wy'east and Klickitat fought over her, blanketing the land with ashes, hot rocks, and lava. Sahale was furious and turned all three of them into mountains: Loowit is Mount St. Helens, Klickitat is Mount Adams, and Wy'east is Mount Hood.

During Capt. George Vancouver's survey of the northwest coast in 1792, he sent Lt. William Broughton with a ship up the Columbia River. From the river, Broughton saw "a very distant high snowy mountain" and named it after Lord Samuel Hood, the Royal Navy admiral who had originally ordered the coastal survey.

In 1803, Pres. Thomas Jefferson sent Meriwether Lewis and William Clark to explore the territory that the United States had recently purchased from France. The expedition canoed down the Columbia River in 1805, wintered near present-day Astoria, and traveled back up the Columbia in 1806. The party explored upstream along the river we now know as the Sandy River and found that the riverbed was "formed entirely of quicksand," which was actually volcanic ash from an eruption that occurred on Mount Hood in the 1790s.

Immigrants started arriving in the area in great numbers in the 1840s. They traveled 2,000 miles over the Oregon Trail in search of a better life, chasing rumors about the fertile farmland in the Willamette Valley. In 1846, Capt. Samuel K. Barlow opened a toll road around the south side of the mountain that served as an alternative to the dangerous route down the Columbia River, albeit an expensive one. Emigrants paid $5 per wagon and $1 per head of stock—an astronomical sum at the time—but that did not stop them from using the toll road. Judge Matthew P. Deady wrote that the road's "construction contributed more toward the prosperity of the Willamette Valley and the future state of Oregon than any other achievement prior to the building of the railways in 1870."

Almost as soon as white settlers started arriving in Oregon, people started trying to climb Mount Hood. Thomas Dryer, owner and editor of the *Oregonian* newspaper, claimed to be the first to summit the mountain in 1854. His account of the climb was so lacking in detail that it is now widely believed that he did not actually succeed in reaching the summit. Credit for the first successful climb of Mount Hood goes to a party of four men—Henry Pittock, Lyman Chittenden, Wilbur Cornell, and Rev. T.A. Wood—who summited on July 11, 1857.

In 1891, the government began to take the first steps to protect the vast amounts of land in the public domain. The Forest Reserve Act allowed the president to set aside forested land as public reservations. This was followed in 1897 by the Organic Act, which dictated how the forest reserves would be managed. Between 1892 and 1907, some 16 forest reserves were set aside in Oregon. The first of these was the Bull Run Reserve, established by Pres. Benjamin Harrison on June 17, 1892.

The growing city of Portland was looking for a water source other than the Willamette River, local creeks, and wells that it had been relying on, and the Portland Water Committee formed in 1885 to establish a municipal water system. It hired an engineer to survey the Bull Run watershed, and in February 1886, Col. Isaac W. Smith led a party into the area. After navigating the rugged terrain and dense vegetation, the men came to pristine Bull Run Lake at the head of the watershed and decided that this was going to be Portland's future water supply.

Twenty-four miles of pipeline had to be constructed to transport water from the Bull Run headworks to the city. On January 2, 1895, Bull Run water flowed into Portland. The designation as a forest reserve prevented human habitation within the watershed, but logging, grazing, mining, hunting, and fishing were still allowed. On April 28, 1904, Pres. Theodore Roosevelt signed into law "An Act for the Protection of the Bull Run Forest Reserve and the sources of the water supply of the City of Portland, State of Oregon" which came to be known as the Bull Run Trespass Act. From that point on, public access to the watershed was banned.

In 1907, the reserves were renamed as national forests, and the Bureau of Forestry became the United States Forest Service (USFS). In 1908, the Bull Run Reserve became part of the newly established Oregon National Forest. The USFS was tasked with protecting the forests from wildfire, and it set about establishing a system of lookout towers, guard stations, and hundreds of miles of telephone lines to achieve that goal.

Most forest rangers were stationed at ranger stations throughout the forest, next to trails, lakes, and rivers. In general, the stations were positioned to be about one day's horseback ride from the next closest station. In the early days, forest rangers earned between $900 and $1,500 per year. They had to provide most of their own equipment—such as bedding, horses, and food—and pay for it themselves. Rangers had a wide variety of duties, including firefighting, staffing fire lookouts, organizing rescue parties for lost hikers, enforcing regulations, providing first aid to the injured, issuing permits for huckleberry picking, and serving as a source of information about everything from hiking trails to the best fishing holes.

A small community established at the southern base of Mount Hood in the late 1800s was known as Government Camp; it was located where a unit of US Army Mounted Riflemen had to abandon some of its wagons in 1848 when its stock became exhausted from traveling the Barlow Road. Oliver Yocum built the Mountain View Hotel in 1900, and when the road to Government Camp was plowed starting in 1927, the little community soon became a mecca for winter sports enthusiasts.

The Columbia River Highway (also known as Highway 30) along the northern edge of the forest was constructed between 1913 and 1922. Residents in Portland and the Willamette Valley had long pushed for better road access to the mountain, and in 1919, construction began on the Mount Hood Loop Highway, which came up from Portland, circled around the south and east sides of the mountain, and met up with the Columbia River Highway in Hood River, where drivers could head west back to Portland. The entirety of the loop was opened to the public on June 25, 1925.

The USFS adopted a policy of removing state names from the names of national forests to avoid confusion, so in January 1924, the Oregon National Forest was renamed the Mount Hood National Forest in honor of the mountain that towers above the forest around it.

The Civilian Conservation Corps (CCC) was a New Deal program established in 1933 to provide jobs during the Great Depression. CCC men who worked in the Mount Hood National Forest fought fires, planted trees, and built ranger stations, guard stations, lookouts, and roads. They also developed many new recreational facilities, including campgrounds, hiking trails, footbridges, and picnic areas. Although they did not know it at the time, the facilities they constructed would come in handy during the postwar recreation boom.

The Works Progress Administration (WPA) was another New Deal program. When plans were finalized to build a lodge on Mount Hood, WPA men were brought in to provide the labor. They broke ground in June 1936, and Timberline Lodge was dedicated by Pres. Franklin D. Roosevelt on September 28, 1937. In 1977, it was declared a National Historic Landmark; it now attracts two million visitors each year.

Fire prevention was a primary concern of the USFS. Major wildfires in 1910 spurred the USFS into action; motivated to protect the valuable timber crop, they established a series of fire lookouts on peaks and mountains across the national forests. The Mount Hood National Forest had more than 100 lookouts over the course of the 20th century, but today, only seven remain, and only four of them are still used for fire-spotting.

The period after World War II saw an increase in recreational use of the national forests. Early roads and trails had been built purely for administrative reasons, but over time they were used more and more by visitors. More people were visiting the forest for fishing, horseback riding, skiing, swimming, and camping. In the late 1940s and 1950s, more campgrounds and other recreational facilities were constructed. Timberline Lodge, which had closed during the war, reopened in December 1945. The first downhill ski area opened at the Summit Ski Area in 1927, and the first chairlift was constructed at Timberline Lodge in 1939. The mountain is now home to five downhill ski areas.

The USFS moved from a custodial role to a management role after World War II, which included timber sales. The price of stumpage—about $2.50 per thousand board feet before the war—jumped to $20 to $25 after the war. Thousands of miles of logging roads were built to access the trees. In the 1950s, there were 1,000 miles of roads in the forest; by 1990, there were 4,000 miles. In 1990, the northern spotted owl was listed as "threatened" under the Endangered Species Act, and logging was drastically reduced as a result.

Starting in the 1960s, special protected areas were set aside as designated wilderness in many national forests. Congress passed the Wilderness Act in 1964, and the 14,160-acre Mount Hood Wilderness was established that year (it has since been expanded to 63,177 acres). The Oregon Wilderness Act was passed in 1984, and four more wilderness areas were established. In 2009, two million acres of new wilderness were designated across nine states, including three new wilderness areas in the Mount Hood National Forest, which now has eight wilderness areas covering more than 300,000 acres.

The Columbia River Gorge National Scenic Area was established in November 1986 after years of debate. The area is 277,000 acres and includes six counties in two states and parts of the Mount Hood National Forest in Oregon and the Gifford Pinchot National Forest in Washington. The scenic area includes waterfalls, wildflower meadows, mountaintop viewpoints, and many miles of hiking trails—it has become an extremely popular destination.

The USFS celebrated its 100th anniversary in 2005. With four million people visiting every year, the Mount Hood National Forest is more popular than ever.

One

THE EARLY YEARS

This 1874 engraving by American landscape painter Robert Swain Gifford depicts Native Americans paddling down the Columbia River. The Chinooks traveled up and down the river in dugout canoes and relied on salmon as a food staple and trade item. They preserved salmon by cutting it into strips and drying it in the sun. (OHS.)

This 1853 lithograph by American artist John Mix Stanley shows Native Americans camped along the Columbia River in sight of Mount Hood. The river—which forms the northern boundary of the Mount Hood National Forest—was an important location for local tribes, who would gather there to fish, trade, and socialize. The forest provided cedar trees, which were used to make mats, capes, skirts, twine, nets, bowls, baskets, canoes, and longhouses. The forest was also a source for berries and wild game. When Lewis and Clark passed through in 1805, they bought dried fish from the natives, who were also able to give the expedition valuable information about the condition of the river ahead. Lewis exchanged one of his smallest canoes for a pine canoe that was lightweight but strong. Clark wrote in his journal that "these canoes are neater made than any I have ever seen." (OHS.)

Native American baskets varied in shape, size, design, and color depending on function. Designs were often passed down within families from one generation to the next. Baskets could be used for gathering and storing roots, berries, camas bulbs, and other food. They were also used for collecting firewood, carrying babies, and in religious ceremonies, as well as given as gifts. (HMHRC.)

This photograph shows an unidentified Native American from the Warm Springs Reservation building a sweat lodge near Zigzag Mountain in the 1930s. Once the sweat lodge was constructed from willow branches and covered with blankets, rocks would be placed in a fire, and when they were hot enough, they would be placed in the sweat lodge. Water would then be poured on the rocks to generate steam. Sweat lodges—used for prayers, rituals, and ceremonial purposes—are still in use today. (George M. Henderson.)

In October 1792, Lt. William E. Broughton left his ship anchored in Astoria Bay while he and his crew rowed up the Columbia River in two boats. He drew on his social connections to give titles to the landmarks he saw along the way, and he named the snowy peak south of the Columbia River after Lord Samuel Hood of the Royal Navy. (CRMM.)

Peter Skene Ogden, a chief trader with the Hudson Bay Company, led a group of trappers and hunters into the Cascade Mountains in 1825. On December 5, the party reached a viewpoint on the east side of Mount Hood where the men could also see Mount Adams, Mount St. Helens, and, to the south, "other lofty mountains in form and shape of sugar loaves." Ogden described it all as "a grand and noble sight." (OHS.)

Capt. Samuel Kimbrough Barlow traveled west on the Oregon Trail in 1845. When his party reached The Dalles, he decided against the dangerous journey down the rapids of the Columbia River in favor of an overland crossing around the south side of Mount Hood, declaring that "God never made a mountain that had no place to go over or around it." The route he established became known as the Barlow Road. (OHS.)

This photograph taken in the 1880s shows a group of men and a mule team posing in front of the fifth and final Barlow Road tollgate. With a hill on one side and a river on the other, it was almost impossible for travelers to continue without passing through the simple wooden gate and paying the toll. Tollgate keeper Daniel Parker planted the two maples flanking the gate in this image. One of the trees and parts of the other still stand over a tollgate replica east of Rhododendron.

Laurel Hill was the most treacherous segment of the Barlow Road. The 60 percent grade was so steep that travelers had to wrap ropes around trees to lower their wagons down the slope. Sometimes the ropes snapped, sending the wagons crashing down the hill. Over 100 years later, the rope burns are still visible on tree stumps.

This tree carving was discovered by a logger near Clackamas Lake in 1959. It reads: "Crawford's Camp, Sept. 25, 1808." Trappers were known to make such carvings as they traveled around the West searching for beavers to meet the high demand back east, but few such carvings have been found. This particular inscription, which was carved out of the tree by the logger and saved by the logging company, can now be seen at the Sandy Historical Society. (Cheryl Hill.)

Perry Vickers was the operator of Summit House, which also served as the Barlow Road tollgate from 1866 to 1870. He was a bighearted man and was always willing to ride out and help travelers in trouble, no matter the hour or the weather. He was the first man to guide climbing parties to the summit of Mount Hood. In August 1883, Vickers joined a posse hunting for a man who had stolen a shotgun. On August 18, when the posse caught up to the thief, he shot Vickers in the stomach before fleeing. As Vickers lay dying that night, he requested to be buried at Summit Meadows. He died at 7:00 the next morning and was buried next to the grave of a nine-month-old baby—the son of W.L. Barclay—who had died while visiting Summit House with his family in September 1882. The tiny cemetery is still visible at the edge of Summit Meadows. Vickers's grave is on the left; the Barclay baby's grave is on the right. (Cheryl Hill.)

Summit Meadows was known as a welcome resting place along the Barlow Road, and from 1866 to 1870 it was the site of the third tollgate, operated by Perry Vickers. By the mid-1880s, it also served as a place for camping and recreation for Portlanders seeking cooler mountain temperatures during the hot summer, as shown in this 1886 picture. (OHS.)

Horace Campbell built a 15-foot-tall cedar shake teepee at Summit Meadows in the 1880s for the enjoyment of campers and recreationists. It had an opening for a door, a fireplace in the center, and a smoke hole at the top. Lige Coalman, who would later become the first fire lookout on the summit of Mount Hood, is the tall man at center wearing a hat.

Two

WORKING IN THE FOREST

Trail crews often had to camp out in the area where they were working, much like this crew pictured on Horseshoe Ridge in 1934. Fire suppression was such a concern that trail crews were equipped with firefighting tools and emergency rations in case they had to deal with a wildfire. So much importance was placed on proper trail construction that the USFS published the 90-page *Forest Trail Handbook* in 1935.

To hasten the regrowth of burned-over forest, Secretary of Agriculture James Wilson ordered the USFS to do direct seeding. In 1911, a seed kiln was constructed at Wyeth along the Columbia River. The crew is pictured here in front of the bin house where thousands of sacks of cones were waiting to be dried and have their seeds shaken out. The kiln ran day and night in three shifts.

The USFS worked on reforesting between 4,000 and 5,000 acres of national forest land in September 1913. Workers planted 3,000 seeds and 800,000 nursery-grown tree seedlings in Oregon and Washington. This photograph shows the camp where men slept and ate while replanting the Still Creek area.

Planting trees was hard work. Men had to forge a way through rough terrain with no trails as they ascended and descended steep hills. They frequently had to crawl over fallen trees or push through thick brush, sometimes in weather that was less than ideal. This crew was working in the Cast Creek area when this picture was taken in 1910.

Snow surveyors measured the depth of the snowpack, as well as its water content. It was important to gather this information to forecast the spring runoff and any potential flooding or drought. Snow surveyors traveled through many miles of remote terrain on skis or showshoes. Because they needed to travel such long distances, they often slept in backcountry cabins and shelters.

David Rose Cooper and his wife, Marion, were Scottish immigrants who settled in the Hood River Valley in 1882. In 1885, they established a tent camp hotel on the mountain near the site where the Cloud Cap Inn would be built four years later. David offered his services as a guide, and Marion cooked the food and helped operate the hotel. This is one of their sons, Warren "Barney" Cooper, who so enjoyed his younger years on the mountain that he became a forest ranger for the Cascade Forest Reserve in the 1890s, before the Mount Hood National Forest was designated. Warren Cooper later served as district ranger for the Hood River Ranger District and, since no ranger station existed, used his home near Parkdale as headquarters. In the early days of the USFS, rangers were expected to possess a large variety of skills, including being able to identify tree and plant species, felling a tree with an axe, operating a compass, using a crosscut saw, building a campfire (and putting it out), and packing a horse.

Albert Wiesendanger, pictured here in 1942, worked for the USFS from 1909 to 1948. He was keen on promoting fire prevention in the forest, and after retiring from the USFS, he served as executive secretary for Keep Oregon Green from 1948 to 1980. In 1998, the Oregon Geographic Names Board named a waterfall along Multnomah Creek for Wiesendanger.

In 1913, the USFS built a guard station at Bagby Hot Springs, a location previously used as a base camp for hunters and miners. The ranger was in charge of station maintenance and collecting twice-daily reports from the nearby fire lookouts. Although the station is no longer in use, it is the oldest known administrative building in the Mount Hood National Forest.

This trapper's cabin was located near Olallie Lake. Trappers were allowed to catch wolves, coyotes, cougars, bears, and other animals in national forests. In some cases, the state or the county would pay bounties for predatory animals such as wolves. In the first decade of the 20th century, a wolf could bring a bounty as high as $50. Rangers were responsible for enforcing trapping and hunting laws.

Sometime prior to 1916, the USFS installed this telephone on the Wapinita Highway (now Highway 26) near Frog Lake. The phone was installed so that passing travelers could report forest fires or car trouble. This particular phone box was painted blue, and although the phone is long gone, its legacy lives on—every day, thousands of vehicles pass over Blue Box Pass on Highway 26.

Fire control and prevention has always been a priority for the USFS. Fire trucks, like this one pictured at the Columbia Gorge Ranger Station in 1924, were only as good as the few roads that gave access into the forest. The USFS established training schools in the 1920s to teach firefighters how to read maps, chase smoke, and detect and fight fires.

Sixty men underwent three days of training at the Bear Springs Guard Station in June 1934. After training for short-term service with the USFS, the men could detect, locate, and suppress forest fires. They could also work at campgrounds and as fire lookouts.

The USFS contains many layers of employees, but the eyes and ears of the agency have always been the forest rangers. In the early days, rangers traveled on foot and often worked in solitude for days on end, but they also had to be good at working with people. They had to fight fires, enforce rules, and warn campers to put out campfires. The jobs of modern rangers are much the same, although present-day transportation, tools, communication, and required skills are vastly different. The ranger pictured in this undated photograph is patroling a trail on horseback.

Before radios, every ranger station, guard station, and lookout was connected to a phone line. Hundreds of miles of no. 9 iron wire were strung throughout the forest and hung with enough slack that if a tree or branch fell on the line, it would sag to the ground but not break. The image at right shows pack animals carrying coils of telephone wire. (George M. Henderson.)

The USFS used telephone lines to communicate with remote guard stations and fire lookouts. When a line became damaged by falling trees or branches, repairmen would travel to it by any means necessary, including skis.

Guard training camp was intense and rigorous, often lasting from dawn to dusk. Guards learned techniques for fighting different kinds of fires—ground fires, crown fires, and lightning-caused fires. They learned how to dig fire lines and knock down flames with dirt. The men practiced on live fires as tanker trucks stood by for backup. These men are receiving training at the Bear Springs Ranger Station in 1937.

Up until 1960, rangers, supervisors, and other employees of the Mount Hood National Forest were sent to "ranger training" or "guard school" at the Region Six Personnel Training Station at Wind River in Washington State. Students learned about fire management, resource management, general administration, and other important topics.

Architect E.U. Blanchfield (left) and Ranger Williamson pose in front of the new shelter at Breitenbush Lake in 1934. The shelter, designed for campers to use, was constructed of a combination of stone and shake. The USFS started developing standards for such buildings in the 1930s, mandating certain materials and paint colors for various types of structures.

In this 1934 photograph, an unidentified patrolman consults a map at the Tilly Jane Guard Station. Patrolmen were responsible for communicating with fire lookouts and district rangers and responding to any wildfires that were spotted. Although patrolmen were trained to fight fires if necessary, their primary goal was to prevent fires in the first place. They were also responsible for monitoring for poaching and other illegal activities.

The Breitenbush Lake Guard Station was built in 1934. Pictured here is a carpenter working on the construction. George Henderson, a USFS employee temporarily stationed at the lake in the early summer of 1936, arrived that year to find that campers, eager to reach the lake and set up, had dug through the last of the winter snowdrifts on the access road and set up camp at prime spots around the lake.

The Mount Hood National Forest contains many miles of hiking trails that require regular maintenance and upkeep. This picture shows members of the Timber Lake Job Corps, which was founded in 1965 to train young men who wanted to learn a trade or skill. The Timber Lake Job Corps center includes seven dormitories, an educational building, an office, a dispensary, a dining hall, and a ball field. The center still operates today.

The USFS built trails in the interests of fire control, administration, grazing, and recreation, and it was hard work. New trails had to avoid boggy areas, creek bottoms subject to flooding, unstable ground, and locations where snowdrifts accumulated. Maintenance was difficult, too. Fallen trees had to be removed, washouts repaired, bridges fixed, and rocks and roots removed.

Demands for new roads increased as more land opened up for logging and recreational opportunities. The men pictured at left are surveying a new road in 1958. Surveying and building roads in the rugged and mountainous terrain could be a challenge. In 1955, some 550 miles of new timber access roads were constructed in the national forests of the Pacific Northwest.

Mud Lake, pictured here, was a swampy area near Summit Meadows. In 1960, the USFS built a 12-foot-tall earth dam and converted this into the 60-acre Trillium Lake. The Forest Service spent $100,000 developing picnic and camping facilities at the new lake, which was stocked with trout and open only to nonmotorized boats.

At left, Summit district ranger Bruce Kirkland is at Trillium Lake speaking to the Mount Hood National Forest Advisory Council, which was formed in 1957 by forest supervisor Lloyd Olson to provide a forum for discussion of policy matters. The lake is still a popular destination for campers, swimmers, boaters, and fishermen and is one of the most photographed spots in the Mount Hood National Forest.

Lookout Dorothy Lynch views the surrounding terrain from Sisi Butte Lookout in this 1951 image. In the first half of the 20th century, hundreds of fire lookouts were built at high points in forests so that the people staffing them could easily spot fires and report them. With technological advancements, most of the fire lookouts in the Mount Hood National Forest are gone, and only a few are still staffed. (MHCCM.)

Fire lookouts like this one on Oak Grove Butte were constructed so that wildfires could be spotted as quickly as possible during the summer fire season. The men and women who worked at fire lookouts were responsible for spotting smoke, getting a fix on its position, and reporting it so that firefighters could respond and extinguish the blaze.

Civilian Conservation Corps enrollee Paul Snyder took this aerial photograph of Camp F-12 from a nearby hill. Camp F-12, one of several CCC camps in the Mount Hood National Forest, was located at Summit Meadows. It was converted into a WPA camp when construction began on Timberline Lodge in 1936.

CCC enrollees in Company 928 were stationed at Camp Zigzag, which operated from 1933 to 1941. The men at this camp were responsible for the construction of the Zigzag Ranger Station, which is now listed in the National Register of Historic Places. This camp also had a sign shop that generated hundreds of signs for roads, trails, and campgrounds.

Enrollees from the Civilian Conservation Corps camp at Zigzag constructed the Tollgate Campground on 12 acres of land along the Zigzag River. They built stone fireplaces and picnic tables for each campsite, as well as a large community picnic shelter. This 1937 photograph shows men working on one of the picnic tables.

CCC Company 697 was based out of Camp Latourell near Bridal Veil. This side camp at Perham Creek was about 40 miles upstream along the Columbia River. The enrollees of Company 697, some of whom are pictured here in July 1934, were assigned to clear snags from past wildfires, build roads, construct trails, and string telephone lines.

During World War II, when many men were called away to the armed services, civilian volunteers were recruited to form the USFS Reserves. Volunteers in the reserves included women, older men (of non-draft age), and high school students. They helped staff lookouts, patrol campgrounds, fight fires, cook for fire crews, or drive fire trucks. This photograph shows reservists training in 1942.

Loggers frequently stood on springboards when felling a tree so that they could start cutting higher on the tree to avoid the butt swell. When the tree began to fall, the men would have to jump down and run. Today, hundreds of stumps throughout the forest still have old springboard notches in them.

This picture shows a road donkey and loading donkey at a logging operation run by the Bridal Veil Lumbering Company near Palmer, Oregon. The intense logging of the early 20th century has declined in recent decades due to environmental restrictions and habitat protection for endangered species such as the northern spotted owl.

Early methods of timber extraction required floating logs to market via log flumes or rivers. Eventually, railroads became the preferred method for moving logs out of the forest. Ironically, the railroads consumed much of the wood that was harvested; firewood powered the locomotives' steam engines, and wood was necessary to build railroad ties, trestles, and train cars.

The timber industry wanted to keep most of the national forests off the market in the first half of the 20th century in order to keep prices elevated. But by the end of World War II, much of the private timber had been harvested, and demand was high thanks to the postwar housing boom, so national forests were opened up to heavier logging.

Logging technology dramatically improved in the 1940s and 1950s with the development of more efficient chain saws and logging railroads being replaced by roads. Suspension systems, used for yarding logs, replaced the steam donkeys that had dragged logs across the ground. Loggers could cut more trees in less time, and clear-cutting became the standard method of logging timber in the 1950s.

Roof shingles made from western red cedar were preferred in the construction industry because of the long-lasting nature of the wood. Portable shingle mills could be easily moved to different logging areas to produce shingles on-site. This 1937 photograph shows a shingle mill at a logging site on Boyer Creek.

Logging was a very dangerous job. Many men who worked in the logging industry drowned on river drives or were killed by falling trees or branches. The advent of more sophisticated logging equipment introduced new kinds of accidents, such as chainsawing injuries. This picture shows a piece of logging equipment that has fallen over.

Counting the rings on a stump tells foresters approximately how old a tree was when it was cut down. Tree rings can also provide information about the environmental history of the area, such as wildfires, insect infestations, droughts, and years of heavy snow or rain.

In the 19th and early 20th centuries, loggers used axes and two-man saws to cut down trees. By the end of World War II, portable gas-powered chain saws were becoming common and allowed loggers to cut down more trees in a shorter amount of time. Despite advances in logging technology and safety equipment, logging is still a dangerous profession.

In 1959, the USFS opened up 42,500 acres of the Bull Run Reserve to the public in response to a growing demand for recreational areas in the forest. The new multiple-use policy adopted by the USFS cleared the way for logging in the watershed. The stump in this 1968 photograph is from a Douglas fir that was approximately 450 years old.

The Knutson-Vandenberg Act, passed in 1930, provided a dedicated fund for reforesting national forest land that had been logged. Under the new law, timber companies were assessed a fee to cover the costs of tree planting after harvest. This photograph shows a man using a soil auger to make a hole in which to plant a tree seedling.

After several incidents involving people getting lost on the mountain, a group of Hood River men recognized the need to create a formal search-and-rescue organization and formed the Crag Rats in 1926. The Crag Rats was an all-volunteer club that evolved from several other groups and clubs; the wife of one member joked that the men spent so much time in the crags that they were like crag rats, and the name stuck. The group is recognized as the oldest search-and-rescue organization in the country. In addition to being physically fit, Crag Rat volunteers have to know how to ski and know how to do technical mountain climbing. They are known for their signature black-and-white checkered shirts. These Crag Rats are doing a snow survey. The Crag Rats use the historic Cloud Cap Inn as a base for training, a headquarters for rescue missions, and a location for holding group meetings. (CR.)

After the completion of Timberline Lodge in 1937, Mount Hood saw an influx of new skiers—and an increase in the number of skiing accidents. Experienced skiers from the Mazamas, the Cascade Ski Club, and other ski groups assisted any injured skiers they passed, but the mountain needed a formal patrol group. With permission from the USFS, the Mount Hood Ski Patrol formed in 1938. The USFS hired Hank Lewis to run the all-volunteer organization. The group still exists and provides rescue and emergency care at four ski areas on the mountain. Members are volunteers who must be experienced skiers and have first aid training. They commit to 15 patrol days each year, along with additional training days to learn about proper sled use, evacuation from chairlifts, and new technologies such as avalanche transceivers.

When the Bull Run Reserve was set aside in 1892 as the source of Portland's drinking water, there was no infrastructure in place to get the water from the mountains to the city. The project required laying 24 miles of riveted steel pipe, which were 33 to 42 inches in diameter, and the removal of all the logs and brush along the 33-foot-wide right-of-way. The conduit and distribution system cost the City of Portland $2.4 million. Bull Run water flowed into Portland for the first time on January 2, 1895. The city was growing fast, so Conduit 2 was completed in 1911, by which time the population of Portland had reached 172,000. With a new dam scheduled to be built, construction on Conduit 3 began in October 1923 and was completed in January 1925. This photograph shows pipe for Conduit 3 being laid across the Sandy River in 1924.

Bull Run Lake is the source of the Bull Run River, which supplies drinking water to the city of Portland. Due to the remoteness of the lake, cabins were constructed on-site to house workers who were building a small dam at the lake in 1917. The cabins are now one of the stops on the daylong watershed tours offered by the Portland Water Bureau.

In 1927, construction began on Dam 1, which impounds 10 billion gallons of water. It cost $3 million and was state of the art for its time. The construction took two years to complete and was plagued with setbacks: two separate wildfires threatened the worker camps, heavy rain in the fall of 1927 destroyed much of the work that had been done as floods also destroyed bridges, and the winter that followed was a severe one.

This photograph shows a subcommittee of the Oregon Geographic Names Board, which made a field inspection in the rugged Salmon River area in the summer of 1963. Seven hard-to-reach waterfalls received official names as a result of the trip: Stein Falls, Split Falls, Hideaway Falls, Little Niagara Falls, Vanishing Falls, Frustration Falls, and Final Falls. The waterfalls are all inside the Salmon-Huckleberry Wilderness, which was established in 1984.

In the first few decades of the USFS, a ranger had to have knowledge of land surveying, logging, trail maintenance, first aid, cooking, and horse skills, among other things. In addition to being strong and fit, rangers were often expected to work from dawn to dusk, sometimes without a day off and often alone.

Three

TRANSPORTATION

This pack train is ready to haul a load of supplies 40 miles to the Oak Grove Ranger Station. Roads were poor or nonexistent in the first few decades of the 20th century, and horses were often the best way to transport people and supplies through the forest. Knowing how to handle horses and mules and how to properly load them was an important job skill. In some areas of the country, pack trains are still used to supply lookouts or other remote stations.

In the early 1900s, there were few roads available to fight fires deep in the forest, and firefighters often had to hike in or ride horses. This 1910 photograph shows a pack train of supplies arriving at the fire lines of the Herman Creek Fire. The second horse is carrying a portable water pump.

Getting tools, food, and supplies for trail construction and maintenance to remote areas usually required the use of horses or mules. This photograph was taken in 1911 at the Little Sandy Guard Station inside the Bull Run Watershed, which, at the time, had very few roads but many miles of trails that were used for patrolling the area.

In the early 1900s, the only land routes across the Cascades in northern Oregon were the old Barlow Road or the Dalles and Sandy Wagon Road along the Columbia River, both of which were rough. Construction on the Columbia River Highway began in 1913. The road was designed by Samuel Lancaster, who modeled it after scenic highways in Europe, especially the Axenstrasse along Lake Lucerne in Switzerland. Lancaster wanted to build a road that was both functional and beautiful, allowing motorists to experience the waterfalls, forests, cliffs, and scenery of the Columbia River Gorge. When the road was completed in 1922, it gave motorists easier access to the northern edge of the Mount Hood National Forest, which was then known as the Oregon National Forest. These motorists are crossing the Shepherd's Dell Bridge; some of them have stopped to admire the waterfall just south of the bridge.

The new Columbia River Highway provided access to viewpoints and scenic spots that most people had never visited. One such spot was Eagle Creek, located a few miles west of the town of Cascade Locks. In the midst of the highway construction, the USFS built a campground at Eagle Creek in 1915; it was the first USFS campground in the country and still exists today. Construction started soon after on a trail that followed Eagle Creek south towards Mount Hood. This photograph shows motorists parked near the entrance of the new campground. The restroom facility in the background—called a comfort station at the time—was later replaced by a larger stone and wood building constructed by the Civilian Conservation Corps.

This photograph shows a car driving along a plank road through Summit Meadows. Wooden planks were laid on the dirt road so that vehicles would be prevented from getting stuck in spring mud. Although plank roads were an improvement over dirt roads, the planks were subject to warping from exposure to the elements. Improvements in highway technology eventually made plank roads obsolete. (OHS.)

This undated photograph shows pack mules hauling supplies to the Mount Hood Fire Lookout. It is unclear if this was during or after the construction of the lookout. It was hard work to get supplies to the summit to construct the lookout and then to keep it supplied with fuel and food. Pack mules could only go so far, and men would have to haul supplies the rest of the way.

This image was taken in September 1920 when Hood River photographer Fred Donnerberg (possibly the man pictured) set out to check on the progress of the road to Lost Lake, which was then under construction. He traveled on an Excelsior motorcycle with a sidecar. The entrance to the Oregon National Forest (not yet renamed Mount Hood National Forest) is marked with this log gateway. (HMHRC.)

Summer recreation cabins existed in the national forest before the 1920s but became popular after the Mount Hood Loop Highway was completed in 1924. Cabins popped up along the highway and its numerous side roads. These people are traveling down a road in the Zigzag area.

In June 1916, the Paige Motor Sales Company in Portland undertook a major publicity stunt by attempting to see how far it could get a Paige Fairfield car up the mountain. A crew of eight men wrestled the car up the mountain from Government Camp through 20 feet of snow. The car had to navigate the steep grade, thick trees, and large boulders, and the men had to cut down trees and build bridges over gullies and dips. At one point, the car slid off one of these improvised bridges and had to be dug out of the snow. One day, the team covered only a quarter mile. A severe summer blizzard forced the entire crew to temporarily abandon the car and retreat to Government Camp, where the men waited for the storm to pass. On July 6, at an elevation of 8,500 feet, they called the stunt a success and headed back down the mountain. (MHCCM.)

The White River is fed by the White River Glacier on Mount Hood and is prone to debris flows and flooding. This 1924 photograph shows a simple wooden bridge crossing the river that could be quickly and easily replaced if it was swept away in a flood. Such a flood occurred in August 1926 as the result of heavy rain and a 50-foot section of the bridge was washed out.

Aneita Brown and her two children were stationed with her husband, ranger Thomas Brown, at the Jordan Creek Guard Station in the 1920s. The guard station was at the eastern edge of the forest, so to visit Aneita's mother in Zigzag—at the western edge of the forest—required a drive along 80 rough and muddy miles of road in this 1919 Dort car. (MHCCM.)

USFS rangers reached their posts by any means necessary, which could mean hiking, riding a horse, or driving. The Lookout Springs Guard Station was located along Abbott Road southeast of Estacada, and this fortunate ranger was able to drive right to his front door in a Ford Roadster.

In 1924, crews were constructing the Mount Hood Loop Highway near Barlow Pass when they came across an unmarked grave. They unearthed a wagon box that held the remains of a pioneer woman who presumably died along the Barlow Road in the 1800s. Her remains were reburied just off the highway, and the spot was marked with a rock cairn and a sign.

Construction on the $2 million Mount Hood Loop Highway began in September 1919. Due to the difficult terrain, construction took five years. Crews had to blast cliffs, construct bridges, and cut down numerous trees to make way for the road. This photograph shows crews working on the stretch between Bennett Pass and Mitchell Creek.

When the Mount Hood Loop Highway was completed in 1925, motorists could drive east from Portland, around the south and east sides of Mount Hood, north to Hood River, then west along the Columbia River back to Portland. A 1926 advertisement in the *Oregonian* newspaper extols the virtues of the highway, noting that "it offers recreation far from clamorous crowds, and sends the visitor home entirely refreshed with the call to come again and again."

In the fall of 1924, crews had just finished working on the new Mount Hood Loop Highway when the first snow fell, so the road was not open to traffic until the following summer. The highway officially opened on June 21, 1925, and at the dedication ceremony, the loop was called a necklace circling the mountain with Portland as the pendant. The entire circuit covered 173 miles. The road's highest point was at Bennett Pass, an elevation of 4,675 feet. This photograph shows a few of the 15,000 eager motorists who drove up to experience the new highway on opening day. Some unmelted winter snow was still around, and some people packed up the snow in boxes to take home with them. Although the highway has since been widened, improved, and straightened, much of the original route is still the same as it was in 1925.

This highway bridge was built near Sahalie Falls in 1928. The 82-foot concrete span crossed the South Fork Hood River near the Mount Hood Meadows Ski Resort along a particularly curvy section of highway. The bridge was bypassed when Highway 35 was straightened and realigned in 1967.

Until the 1930s, the only way to reach the summit of Larch Mountain was via trail. In 1937, Brower Road was extended 10.5 miles so that motorists could drive from the Columbia River Highway to the Larch Mountain summit. Works Progress Administration workers provided the labor during construction. The new road was formally dedicated during a ceremony on August 3, 1939, which was attended by nearly 500 people.

Prior to World War II, the Clackamas River area south of Estacada had no roads, and the only access was via a narrow gauge railroad. The railroad, pictured here in 1923, had been built by Portland General Electric to serve the Three Lynx hydroelectric power plant, and the USFS was allowed to use the line to transport freight and passengers to the district headquarters near the plant. (George M. Henderson.)

Civilian Conservation Corps men built a lot of new infrastructure in the Mount Hood National Forest during the 1930s. This suspension bridge over the Clackamas River was constructed in 1934 by enrollees of CCC Camp 1 1/2. The 210-foot bridge cost $20,000 to build.

District ranger Joe Graham had to get material to the top of Mount Wilson for a new fire lookout in 1923. There was only a rough trail to the summit, so he improvised. A 10-ton tank hauled two heavy wagons loaded with construction material, and just enough trees were cleared to let it through. Along with engineer John Sinclair and brakeman Ben Richardson, Graham made it to the top without incident.

This photograph shows crews working on construction of Forest Road 58. Mount Hood and Wolf Peak are visible in the background. Roads like this were built to move people and goods from one place to another, to provide logging trucks with access to timberlands, and to allow access for rangers, guards, and firefighters who were protecting the valuable trees.

The Oregon Skyline Trail was a predecessor to the Pacific Crest Trail trail that traveled along the Cascade Mountains of Oregon. The Skyline Trail formally opened in 1921, and newspaper articles extolled the scenic wonders, sweeping vistas, and beautiful lakes along the route. Automobiles were becoming more common, however, and work began soon after on a road following roughly the same route. This 1922 photograph shows a converted World War I tank and a grader working on the construction of the road between the Clackamas Lake Ranger Station and Lemiti Ranger Station. The road was known as Skyline Road, named after the trail that it superseded. The road is still used today to access the Olallie Lake area.

The USFS issued a special use permit in 1947 to the Mount Hood Aerial Transportation Company, headed by Dr. J. Otto George and A.L. Greenwalt, to build an aerial tram between Government Camp and Timberline Lodge. The Skiway aerial tram opened in 1951 after two years of summer-only work to erect the 40 towers that supported the cables. The lower terminal was at the Thunderhead Inn in Government Camp, and the upper terminal was just west of Timberline Lodge. The tram cars—converted city buses—carried people three miles up the mountain to Timberline Lodge for a 75¢ fee. Taking the shuttle bus up the newly improved road to the lodge was faster and cheaper, though, so the tram was a money-loser and closed after only a few years. The towers were taken down in 1961.

Today, the highways to Mount Hood are regularly plowed, but that was not always the case. In January 1926, George Keep, the manager of the Portland branch of the Moreland Motor Truck Company, decided to show off one of his trucks. He sent a Moreland snowplow loaded with five tons of gravel to plow the road up to Government Camp and a few miles beyond to the Wapinita Highway, where a turnaround loop was plowed for drivers. Winter road access was such a novelty that 3,000 motorists drove up to Government Camp the next day just because they could; many people brought skis and toboggans. The next winter, the Oregon State Highway Commission started plowing the road. This picture shows plowing at Timberline Lodge, which receives an average of 500 inches of snow each winter. Government Camp gets an average of 300 inches of snow each winter.

Heavy rains in December 1964 caused flooding along Oregon waterways, including the Clackamas River. A chunk of Highway 224 south of Estacada was washed away by the floodwaters, and a landslide in the same spot covered most of the rest of the remaining road.

When 4.2 inches of rain fell in a 24-hour period in November 1969, the White River flooded and washed out a chunk of Highway 35 that was 30 feet wide and 25 feet deep. During the night, two unsuspecting drivers plunged into the washout. Although some people were injured, none of the drivers or passengers were killed.

Four

RECREATION

Lost Lake got its name in 1880 when a party of men from Hood River who were trying to locate the lake had trouble finding it due to wildfire smoke. A road to the lake was built in the early 1920s, and eventually a store, cabins, and a campground were constructed there. Every summer, thousands of people come to Lost Lake to camp, fish, picnic, and hike.

After their June 1919 conference in Portland, 350 Greeters of America embarked on an automobile tour of the Columbia River Highway. At lunchtime, they gathered at Eagle Creek for a salmon bake, where 17 Chinook salmon were prepared by the head chef of the Hotel Portland. Gov. Ben Olcott and forest supervisor T.H. Sherrard spoke about the beauty of Oregon while the group enjoyed its lunch.

This 1941 photograph shows a group from an organizational camp taking a hike in the Bear Springs area. Recreational use of national forests diminished during World War II, but people had more leisure time—and the number of national forest visitors increased—during the prosperous postwar period.

In the summer of 1921, Hood River resident C. Edward Graves set out to explore the area on the north side of Mount Hood. With him were three friends who also loved the mountains: a high school teacher and an orchardist and his wife. The four followed a poorly marked trail up the mountain and found their way to Dollar Lake, where they camped. From there, they explored Barrett Spur and Coe and Ladd Glaciers, from which they could see a large green meadow below them. They set off to find the meadow and discovered "extensive gardens" of wildflowers with a cascading mountain stream flowing through them. They were so enchanted with the place that they named it Eden Park. In the 1930s, the Civilian Conservation Corps constructed the Timberline Trail just above the meadow. The horseback riders pictured here are camping at Eden Park.

Huckleberry-picking was a popular activity during the 1930s. Berries could be sold at market for 50¢ per gallon, which helped many families supplement their incomes during the hard times of the Great Depression. The photograph above shows berry-pickers stopping at the Summit Meadows Guard Station to get berry-picking permits. Newspaper reports kept people updated about the status of each year's crop, provided maps depicting the best picking locations, and informed people about where permits could be obtained.

In 1926, the USFS built the campground at Tilly Jane, complete with cookstoves crafted from native mountain rock. The Civilian Conservation Corps, in anticipation of increased use of this area, enlarged and improved the campground in 1934. These campers are enjoying a meal at the Tilly Jane campground in 1935.

Recreational facilities built by the Civilian Conservation Corps in the 1930s served the public well after the war, but by the 1960s, the facilities were falling into disrepair. The USFS built new campgrounds, some of which had kitchen shelters, fish-cleaning stations, and flushable toilets. The USFS also started charging a fee at some sites, which it had never done before.

The USFS swiftly recognized the construction of summer homes as a legitimate recreational use of national forests. Visitors started building summer homes in the Mount Hood National Forest around 1915, when Congress enacted the Term Occupancy Act. One such home is pictured in this undated photograph. The number of summer homes increased dramatically in the 1920s, with most concentrated in the Rhododendron area. Some of the summer homes around Mount Hood were built by Henry Steiner, a German immigrant, and his eldest son, John. The Steiners built their cabins in the architectural style known as Oregon Rustic. They always used native trees and stone to build their cabins and often used bent or twisted trees for railings, doors, and furniture. John was known for his fireplaces, which were always perfectly proportioned. Many of the Steiner cabins still stand today.

A group completed the first ascension of Mount Hood via the south side on July 11, 1857. The group consisted of Henry Pittock, Lyman Chittenden, Wilbur Cornell, and Rev. T.A. Wood. Reverend Wood later wrote in his diary: "Never in all my life have I seen a grander or more impressive sight." In those days before sunscreen, all four men ended up with bad sunburns from their expedition. The route up the south side was the first one to be explored, but as climbing became more popular, more routes were established. Today, the south side route climbs 5,000 feet from Timberline Lodge to the summit and is the most popular way to ascend the mountain. Part of the route travels along a ridge known as the Hogsback, a high ridge of snow near Crater Rock, pictured here in 1963. About 10,000 people attempt to climb Mount Hood each year, making it one of the most-climbed volcanic peaks in the world.

The climbing group that would become known as the Mazamas formed on July 19, 1894. On that day, climbers answered an announcement in the *Oregonian* to organize a climbing group on Mount Hood. The advertisement reads, in part: "The list of charter members will be limited to those then and there present, and no one will be permitted to join thereafter except such as have climbed to the summit of an acceptable snow-capped mountain." (To this day, this is still a requirement to join.) That day, 105 charter members joined the group. The name of the group comes from the Spanish word for mountain goat. Mount Mazama—the ancient volcano in southern Oregon that contains Crater Lake—is named for the group. Today, the Mazamas organizes more than 300 different climbs each year for more than 3,000 members, such as the climb pictured in this undated photograph.

Snowshoes have been around for thousands of years. They were originally used in the national forest purely for transportation purposes, so that rangers or other personnel could travel by foot in the winter. But snowshoes have become popular among people who want to hike in the snow or who want to access backcountry ski areas.

Two climbers stand on the Eliot Glacier in this undated photograph. The Eliot Glacier is on the northeast side of Mount Hood and is one of 12 glaciers on the mountain. As of 2004, it covered 395 acres, having lost about 19 percent of its mass since 1901.

The snowmobile was invented to address the need for transportation in snowy areas because regular vehicles could not handle deep snow. Although it was originally built for utilitarian purposes, the snowmobile became popular for recreational use in the 1960s. Snowmobilers who visit Mount Hood enjoy traveling the miles of snow-covered forest roads that are closed to cars in the winter.

In this 1969 photograph, cross-country skiers and a snowmobile pass each other on a snowy forest trail. Cross-country skiing originated in Europe and arrived in North America in the 1800s. Although cross-country skis are still used for transportation in snow, they are also widely used for recreation and sport.

After 1945, the USFS started to build more campgrounds in response to increasing demand for recreational facilities. Recreational vehicles (RVs) became a popular way to enjoy campgrounds because they were ideally suited for families who wanted to experience nature but still have access to modern conveniences.

Today, Elk Meadows can only be reached by trail, but it almost had a highway built right through it. When the Mount Hood Loop Highway was being surveyed in 1915, residents of Hood River wanted the road to go through Elk Meadows because of the spectacular scenery and mountain views. The plan never materialized, and Elk Meadows is now within the protected Mount Hood Wilderness area.

The Civilian Conservation Corps built the Timberline Trail—a 41-mile trail circling Mount Hood—in the 1930s. Hiking the entire loop continues to be a popular backpacking trip. In this 1968 photograph, backpackers stand at the rim of Zigzag Canyon, located two miles west of Timberline Lodge.

In August 1964, some 90 Girl Scouts and their leaders headed to the Mount Hood National Forest. The USFS assisted with the training program, which was meant to teach the girls primitive camping and backpacking skills. Some of the girls stayed at camp to receive conservation training and go on field trips, while the rest embarked on a 40-mile, five-day backpacking trek.

Chinidere Mountain, where the hiker pictured above is resting, was named for the last reigning chief of the Wasco tribe and stands near Wahtum Lake on the north side of Mount Hood. The mountain is 4,674 feet tall and provides a breathtaking view of several Cascade peaks. Chinidere Mountain was once the site of a fire lookout, which was removed in the 1940s. In May 1916, construction began on the Eagle Creek Trail starting at the Columbia River Highway and following Eagle Creek 14 miles south to Wahtum Lake. Some sections required workers to blast rock from the sheer cliffs to make way for the trail, as shown at right. When the trail was completed in 1917, it allowed hikers to connect with the Herman Creek Trail and hike a loop.

In April 1915, the USFS surveyed a trail from Multnomah Falls to the summit of Larch Mountain, from which five Cascade peaks are visible. The USFS began work that spring and completed the trail in September. The trail was the only way to reach the summit until a the completion of a road in 1939, when the drive up Larch Mountain immediately became so popular that the USFS had to expand the parking lot.

The Columbia River forms the northern boundary of the Mount Hood National Forest in an area known as the Columbia River Gorge. Hiking trails in the Gorge are at the lowest elevation in the forest and therefore provide year-round hiking opportunities. This undated photograph shows a man pointing out the Multnomah Falls trailhead on a wooden sign.

The USFS banned motorboats at Olallie Lake and at Breitenbush in 1936. Although some boaters were not happy with the restriction, most people were fine with the new rule. One lake user wrote a letter to the USFS, commenting: "I know of no noise that is more disturbing than the din of an outboard motor."

These three children on horseback have stopped to look at the sign at the Lost Creek Campground. In 1983, volunteers from International Mobility and the Handicapped Sportsmen's Club provided the labor to build a campground with handicapped access at Lost Creek.

Zigzag Mountain provides such a commanding view of the surrounding landscape that it was once home to two different lookouts, one on the east summit (at 4,971 feet) and one on the west summit (at 4,468 feet). The lookouts are long gone, but the views can still be enjoyed by hikers.

The Pacific Crest National Scenic Trail covers more than 2,500 miles and runs from the Mexican border to the Canadian border. The idea for the trail was proposed in the 1920s, but the trail was not officially completed until 1993. The Oregon section of the trail travels along the Cascade Mountains, and the final portion passes through the Mount Hood National Forest before crossing the Columbia River into Washington. (Cheryl Hill.)

From left to right, George M. Henderson, Foster Steele, Bud Waggener, Ralph Day, and Everett Lynch pose for this photograph at Blue Box Pass before beginning an 80-mile ski trip down the Skyline Trail in February 1936. They had to take turns breaking trail in the new snow, all while carrying heavy packs. The weather was so cold that the men were at risk for frostbite, and one night, Henderson had to thaw a frozen thumb in warm water. Their trek was supposed to end at the Detroit Ranger Station, but Steele broke his leg near Breitenbush Hot Springs. With the help of the others, he managed to shuffle along until they reached the springs. The men used the phone at the hot springs to call for help, and the group was transported out after a snowplow cleared the road for a rescue truck. (George M. Henderson.)

Everett Sickler developed the ski jump on Multorpor Mountain in 1928, and in January 1929, the Cascade Ski Club sponsored the jump's first tournament, which was attended by 3,500 spectators. The Multorpor Ski Area, established nearby in the late 1930s, merged with Skibowl on the adjacent property in 1964. The entire complex is now known as Mount Hood Skibowl, which provides the largest night-skiing area in America.

When Timberline Lodge opened in 1937, skiers flocked to the mountain even though it did not have a chairlift. Skiers skied down the mountain to Government Camp and either caught a ride or hiked back up to the lodge. The Magic Mile, the first chairlift on Mount Hood, opened in 1939.

In 1937, the Mount Hood Winter Sports Association built a rope tow at the base of Tom Dick and Harry Mountain in the area that would later become Mount Hood Skibowl. With the postwar surge in skiing, the Multorpor Mountain Company constructed the first chairlift in 1946, and in 1964, the company merged operations with the neighboring Skibowl. Skibowl now has four chairlifts and 960 acres of skiable terrain.

Trillium Lake was a marsh known as Mud Lake until it was dammed and renamed in 1960. With easy access from Highway 26 and up-close views of Mount Hood, the lake is a popular spot for camping, picnicking, swimming, boating, and fishing. The 57-acre lake is open to only nonmotorized boats and is stocked with rainbow trout every year.

This photograph shows two fishermen showing off their catch along the banks of Still Creek. Still Creek originates from the Palmer Glacier, high up on the south side of Mount Hood above Timberline Lodge, where year-round skiing is available. The creek's name comes from pioneers, who noted the relative quietness of this stream in comparison with the turbulent Zigzag River.

This 1959 photograph shows a fisherman along the Clackamas River, a popular place for steelhead and salmon fishing. Fishermen who prefer lake fishing can visit one of the lakes stocked by the Oregon Department of Fish and Wildlife. Lakes were sometimes stocked by hauling special cans via pack train. Today, the ODFW often uses helicopters to dump fish into a lake from the air.

In June 1968, the first lady, Lady Bird Johnson, visited Oregon to address the American Institute of Architects convention in Portland. She also visited Mount Hood, stopping on the way at the Tollgate Campground for a picnic. Along with Zigzag district ranger Dick Buscher (left) and USFS chief Ed Cliff, she dined on grilled Oregon salmon, coleslaw, potato salad, corn on the cob, and huckleberry pie.

Lady Bird Johnson (seated at left center) was scheduled to go on a five-mile hike during her visit to Mount Hood. But the weather was cloudy and wet, and the hike was canceled. Instead, she and Secretary of Agriculture Orville Freeman (to her left) watch a backpacking demonstration by Zigzag district ranger Dick Buscher (man with backpack). Despite the bad weather that day, she is quoted in the *Oregonian* newspaper as saying that "Oregon is simply beautiful."

Five

PLACES

The Lemiti Ranger Station, shown here in 1934, was located in the southern part of the Mount Hood National Forest at the base of Lemiti Butte. It was positioned along the Skyline Trail, which was completed in 1921. The trail was turned into a road in the 1920s, and this structure eventually disappeared. *Lemiti*, Chinook Jargon for mountain, is included in the name of a meadow, creek, and butte at this spot.

The USFS built the Walker Prairie Guard Station inside the Bull Run Watershed in 1909, the same year this photograph was taken. It was one of several stations used by rangers who patrolled the watershed, which was (and still is) the source of Portland's drinking water and therefore closed to the public. Rangers traveled 100 miles of trails to keep an eye out for forest fires and unauthorized campers, hikers, hunters, and fishermen.

The Civilian Conservation Corps built the Bear Springs Guard Station in the 1930s using the same plans that were utilized to build the Honeymoon Cabin at the Clackamas Lake Ranger Station. Thanks to the urging of protective assistant Alton Everest, the station included a shower and toilet.

The USFS built this station in 1935 along the Sandy River on the west slope of Mount Hood. It was intended to house a guard who would keep people from wandering off the Timberline Trail and illegally entering the closed Bull Run Watershed, the source of drinking water for the city of Portland. After 1942, the building was no longer staffed, and it now sits abandoned within the borders of the Mount Hood Wilderness.

The Upper Barlow Guard Station, pictured here in 1943, was located along the old Barlow Road in Devil's Half Acre Meadow. Diaries from Oregon Trail pioneers who traveled the Barlow Road mention an area devastated by a wildfire that was referred to as the Big Deadening. The scorched stumps and snags from that fire may be the origin of the name Devil's Half Acre.

The Civilian Conservation Corps built the Zigzag Ranger Station in the 1930s. The station consists of a trails warehouse, a carpenter shop, a maintenance building, a ranger's residence, and other buildings; it has been in continuous use since it opened. It currently serves as the administrative headquarters for the Zigzag Ranger District.

This new visitor's center opened at the Zigzag Ranger Station in 2013. Offices previously located on both sides of the highway were moved into the center. Visitors can peruse interpretive displays and find information on roads, trails, recreational opportunities, area attractions, lodging, shopping, and dining. (Cheryl Hill.)

Civilian Conservation Corps men from Camp Dee built the Parkdale Ranger Station around 1933. It included a ranger's residence, a garage, shops, and warehouses. This is the ranger's office where the district ranger worked when he was not out in the field. The complex has since been converted to the Parkdale Work Center and was listed in the National Register of Historic Places in 1986.

In 1974, the USFS built the Hood River Ranger Station along Highway 35 south of Hood River. It serves as the administrative headquarters for the Hood River Ranger District and is an information center for visitors approaching the forest from Hood River. The newly remodeled and expanded visitor's center (pictured) opened in 2013.

In the 1930s, the Civilian Conservation Corps built the Oak Grove Ranger Station (pictured here in 1935) south of Estacada. Until a road was built, the only way to reach the station from Estacada was by train or horse. The USFS converted it to a work center in the 1960s. The site has since been abandoned. (OHS.)

In 1905, the USFS established a ranger station at Clackamas Lake; district ranger Joe Graham built the structure. The Civilian Conservation Corps greatly expanded the compound in the 1930s with the addition of a mess hall, a blacksmith shop, a fire warehouse, a horse barn, a roads and trails warehouse, and other buildings. The ranger's office (pictured) still stands, along with several other buildings.

In the 1920s, before a resort existed in the area, the USFS built a guard station at Lost Lake. Despite the lack of a developed campground, people still drove out to the lake to camp. The ranger on duty had to keep the peace and even made a few arrests when campers chopped down trees or were careless with campfires.

The USFS built this cabin at Olallie Meadow in 1910. It originally served as a ranger station and was later used as lodging for fire guards, then as quarters for trail crews. In 2002, volunteers put a new roof on the cabin and did other restoration work. For a while, the cabin was offered for rent through the nearby Olallie Lake Resort, but it now stands abandoned.

The resort of Swim, also known as Mount Hood Mineral Springs, was established near Government Camp in the early 1920s. Boyd Summers, who ran the resort, was named postmaster when a post office opened in 1925. The resort offered fishing, hiking, campgrounds, a store, cabins, and "hot tub baths of radioactive mineral water." A large concrete pool of warm water was the crowning feature of Swim. The Great Depression caused the resort to shut down sometime after 1935, and the buildings were removed by the USFS. A hot spring has never been located at the site, leading to speculation that Summers heated the water artificially.

The small community of Government Camp was a summer-only destination until the late 1920s, when the Oregon State Highway Commission decided to start plowing the highway in winter. Thousands of visitors drove up in the winter to ski or just play in the snow. This 1949 photograph shows the main street through town clogged with cars and people.

The Mountain View Inn, Battle Axe Inn, and Hill's Place are visible in this 1946 street scene from Government Camp. The main street through town was Highway 26, which was later rerouted along the edge of town. The town gets its name from an 1849 incident in which a small command of US Army Mounted Riflemen had to abandon some of its wagons along the Barlow Road because the horses and mules were exhausted.

Everett Sickler purchased land in Government Camp in 1925 and constructed the Battle Axe Inn. It had a large fireplace in the eclectic main room, homemade chairs and furniture, a lunch counter (below), and guest rooms upstairs. Sickler and his wife, Belle, ran the inn with Bud and Irene Flurry. A three-story Recreational Building was later built up the street, but when running the business became difficult during the Great Depression, the Recreational Building was moved and attached to the inn (shown above). The inn installed a toboggan slide nearby, but—although it was popular—accidents were common and insurance grew too costly, so the slide was shut down. The Battle Axe Inn was bought and sold several times over the years and finally burned down in 1950.

M-615 Fountain and Lunch Counter, Battle Axe Inn — Government Camp, Ore.

Oliver Yocum built the 16-room Mountain View Hotel at Government Camp in 1900. Guests could hire Yocum as a mountain guide if they wished to summit Mount Hood. Lige Coalman bought the Mountain View Hotel in 1910 and built a larger hotel next door, which opened in 1912. The two buildings became known as the Government Camp Hotel. With a capacity of 50 guests, it was the primary lodging place in town. The entire hotel burned down on October 11, 1933, when a fire started in the attic and quickly spread. The fire was so intense that it threatened neighboring buildings.

In 1924, Albert Furlong and his wife, Betsy, set up a hot-dog stand along Highway 26 near the Mazama Lodge east of Rhododendron. They received enough business that they decided to build a permanent establishment and erected the two-story Oregon Trail Tavern in 1925. The lower floor housed the restaurant, along with a huge native-stone fireplace. The second floor had rooms for the family plus one to rent. The Furlongs also built three cabins to rent to tourists and sold gasoline to passing motorists. Betsy bought huckleberries from Native Americans, using them to bake her famous huckleberry and lemon custard pies. The tavern closed down sometime in the early 1940s, and the Oregon City Ski Club used the building for a few years after that. The structure still stands and is now part of the Paradise Trail Camp.

Former Portland mayor Henry S. Rowe built the Rhododendron Inn in 1905 in the small community of Rhododendron. The inn had 14 guest rooms, a dining hall, and cottages. When Emil and Suzette Franzetti bought the place in 1912, they added a dance hall, a swimming pool, a tennis court, a croquet court, and cabins. They also built an annex across the highway with eight additional rooms and a dining room, plus cottages and tent houses. Because the Franzettis operated a formal establishment—which is pictured here in 1925—they attracted wealthy guests. Thomas Rex bought the hotel in 1948, renamed it Rex Inn, and closed it over the winter for renovations. When the pipes froze during a cold snap in February 1949, a worker thawing them out with a blowtorch accidentally started a fire; the inn burned to the ground and was never rebuilt.

This building was constructed in 1937 along Highway 26 as a garage for Timberline Lodge. In 1952, the Commercial Club of Portland converted it into Snow Bunny Lodge, a place where families could sled, play in the snow, and enjoy a hot meal. In the early 1990s, asbestos, dry rot, and electrical problems proved too costly to fix, and the building was torn down in 1992.

The USFS built this stone shelter for climbers in 1934. It was located on the east side of Crater Rock, 1,500 feet below the summit of Mount Hood. The expansion of the freezing moisture in the walls and the slowly shifting ground beneath created cracks in the shelter's walls, and it crumbled to the ground within a few years.

Lige Coalman (pictured at left along with an unidentified man in this 1922 photograph) was the first fire lookout on Mount Hood during the summer of 1915, and his only protection from the elements was a 12-foot-by-12-foot tent. During construction of a summit cabin that fall, Coalman and Roy Mitchell were stuck in their tent for three days and two nights during a storm so severe that they eventually had to cut through 30 inches of ice to escape from their tent.

The fire lookout on the summit of Mount Hood, pictured here in 1926, was one of the first lookouts built in Oregon. Conditions on the summit could be extremely harsh, even in summer, and the USFS felt that it was too high for practical use, so 1933 was the last year that the lookout was staffed. The building slipped off the north face of the mountain in 1941.

When the Civilian Conservation Corps built the Timberline Trail encircling Mount Hood in the 1930s, it also built a series of six stone shelters. The shelters served as places where hikers could rest or seek shelter from bad weather. At left is the shelter on Cooper Spur, located above the Cooper Spur Ski Area. It sits 6,700 feet up on the northeast side of the mountain and is one of only three stone shelters still standing. Until it was destroyed by a falling tree in 1994, the shelter pictured below was located at Paradise Park, a five-mile hike west of Timberline Lodge.

Camp Chinidere, a Boy Scout camp, opened in 1916 at Wahtum Lake. Any Boy Scout in good standing could stay at the camp for $5 per week. The Boy Scouts rode the train from Portland to Eagle Creek and then hiked 14 miles to the camp. Their supplies and luggage continued on the train to Cascade Locks and were brought in by pack animals via the Herman Creek Trail. The camp had a capacity of 150 Scouts, who learned to swim, went on hikes, rode horses, and fished for trout in the lake. A swimming instructor and athletic director created a detailed daily program of activities, rest, and recreation for the boys. All of the camp work—except for the cooking—was done by the boys; two cooks stayed busy making three meals per day for the campers. The boys' fathers could visit any time and even stay over for one night, but any other visitors were only allowed on Sundays.

In 1889, Portland banker William M. Ladd and attorney C.E.S. Wood built Cloud Cap Inn at an elevation of 5,900 feet on the slopes of Mount Hood. Designed by Portland architect William H. Whidden, it cost $50,000 to build and was the first recreational resort on the mountain. The construction crew for Cloud Cap Inn consisted of men from Hood River. Logs were hewn and dragged to the site before being bolted together. One of the fireplaces, built from rock taken from nearby cliffs, is pictured below. Water was piped to the inn from a spring. Workers camped at a place known as Roaring Camp, north of the inn. (Above, courtesy HMHRC; below, courtesy USFS.)

During Cloud Cap Inn's first full season in 1890, only 88 guests stayed there. Ladd and Wood turned over operation of the inn to Sarah Langille in 1891. Pictured above are four small cabins that were built around 1900 near Cloud Cap Inn for visitors to rent. Homer Rogers from Parkdale bought the inn in 1919, and it changed hands several times in the next 20 years until the final owner, Boyd French Sr., closed it down at the start of World War II. The USFS bought the inn in 1942. It issued a permit to the Crag Rats mountain rescue group in 1954 to use the building as a base for training, rescue missions, and group meetings. The Crag Rats still use it today. The inn, pictured below in 1952, came close to burning down when a 2008 wildfire came within 30 feet of the building.

The Civilian Conservation Corps built this ski shelter in 1939. It had a kitchen and dining hall on the ground floor and a sleeping area in the loft. The Tilly Jane Ski Trail leading to the Cooper Spur Ski Area ran directly past the shelter. The name Tilly Jane came from the nearby creek, which was named after the wife of William Ladd, the man who built Cloud Cap Inn.

J. Wesley Ladd, uncle of William M. Ladd, invited some guests for a winter outing at Cloud Cap Inn in 1904. They had such a good time that they formed a group that they called the Snowshoe Club. Their annual outings were so successful that they signed a 99-year lease with the USFS and built this lodge north of Cloud Cap Inn.

Robert Bagby was a trapper and miner who discovered hot springs in the forest in 1881. Bagby Hot Springs was used for years before a bathhouse and soaking tubs were built in 1939. A channel was chiseled out of the rock to direct the 136-degree water into a log trough to the bathhouse, where bathers could control the flow of water into tubs. With no electricity available, bathers often used candles for illumination when visiting at night. The bathhouse burned down in 1979 due to an unattended candle. The USFS wanted to close the site but issued a permit for the nonprofit Friends of Bagby group to rebuild the bathhouse, re-create the 10-foot-long cedar tubs, and construct a large, round communal tub in the open air. In 2012, the USFS contracted with a private concessionaire to operate and maintain the hot springs.

The Mazamas built a lodge at Twin Bridges, near Rhododendron, in 1923. Although it was along the road to Government Camp, it was past the point where snowplows went in winter, which assured the Mazamas that they could ski to their lodge from Rhododendron and enjoy some solitude. The road was plowed for winter use starting in 1927, and the Mazamas built a new lodge in Government Camp in 1931.

The Mazamas built this lodge at Government Camp in 1931. It had dormitories that held 100 people, two kitchens, a ski-waxing room, and a fireplace with stones engraved with the names of many Pacific Northwest outdoor clubs. On December 4, 1958, an electrical short caused a fire that burned the lodge to the ground. A new lodge, built in 1959, still stands today.

The United States celebrated its 200th birthday in 1976. Many programs and events were planned for the celebration, and one of the ideas included a wagon train. This idea evolved into five wagon trains that followed historic trails and wagon routes as they headed to Pennsylvania, where they were scheduled to arrive on July 4, 1976. Every state was represented by its own wagon. The Northwest wagon train started at the Peace Arch in Blaine, Washington, on June 8, 1975. It headed south before turning east, traveling the Barlow Road in reverse. The wagons shown here are traveling the old Barlow Road through the Mount Hood National Forest before continuing east to (approximately) follow the route of the Oregon Trail in reverse. After traveling 3,000 miles over 14 months, the wagon train reached Valley Forge, Pennsylvania, on July 4, 1976.

Replacing an earlier 100-foot-tall tower that was built in 1933, this 41-foot-tall fire lookout was built on Hickman Butte on the west side of Mount Hood by the USFS in 1953. This lookout is inside the boundaries of the Bull Run Watershed and is still staffed every summer. It is one of only seven lookout towers still standing in the Mount Hood National Forest.

The first Bull of the Woods lookout, built by the USFS in 1923, was replaced with this tower in 1942. In the 1960s, it ceased to be used as a lookout, but the tower still stands and now sits in the Bull of the Woods Wilderness, which was established in 1984. It is available for visitors to use for free on a first-come, first-served basis.

This unusual fire lookout was established by the USFS on Larch Mountain in 1914. Two 90-foot-tall tree trunks supported a platform from which the forest could be watched for wildfires. This photograph was taken in 1922—the year before the lookout was replaced with a steel lookout tower. The steel tower was replaced with a timber tower in the 1940s, and the timber tower was torn down in 1976.

The 7,215-foot-tall Olallie Butte towers over Olallie Lake at the southern end of the Mount Hood National Forest. This picture shows nearby Mount Jefferson and, in the distance, the trio of mountains known as the Three Sisters. The fire lookout on Olallie Butte was built in 1920 and used until the 1960s.

Multnomah Falls became a popular destination for motorists after the Columbia River Highway opened in 1915. The waterfall—Oregon's tallest—drops more than 600 feet in two tiers. The City of Portland built the Multnomah Falls Lodge in 1925 to capitalize on the booming tourist trade. It still stands today.

Vista House sits at Crown Point high above the Columbia River. Portland architect Edgar Lazarus designed the house, and construction was completed on it in 1918. It was intended to be a place where travelers could admire the views of the Columbia River Gorge and reflect on the pioneers who struggled to make it down the river on the last leg of the Oregon Trail journey.

The Civilian Conservation Corps built the 400-square-foot warming hut at Mount Hood Skibowl in 1936. In 1939, a rope tow was installed from the bottom of the hill up to the warming hut, giving skiers easier access. Coffee, snacks, and soft drinks were available for purchase, and a series of stone stoves spread warmth throughout the building. (Cheryl Hill.)

In this 1953 image, John Todd (left) and E. Peffer survey Bull Run Lake from Hiyu Mountain. The watershed of the Bull Run River was set aside in 1895 as a source of drinking water for Portland, located 26 miles to the west. Although the water is treated before it reaches people's homes, the watershed is closed to the public to protect the quality of the water.

The Blue Bucket Inn was built along Highway 35 around 1925. The inn was run by Lillie and Irma Bowerman and provided rental cabins, meals, groceries, and gas. The inn closed during World War II due to gas shortages; it never reopened after the war and was later demolished.

George and Jennie McMullin opened the Mount Hood Tavern in 1927 at the corner of Cloud Cap Road and Cooper Spur Road. It had a gift shop, a snack bar, a restaurant, three rustic cabins, and gasoline pumps. In 1945, the McMullins sold it to Kenneth and Kathryn See, who changed the name to Tamarack Lodge and operated it until about 1958. It is no longer open to the public, but the buildings still stand.

Six

TIMBERLINE LODGE

Timberline Lodge, built between 1936 and 1938, was a Works Progress Administration project. This photograph was taken sometime before the 1939 construction of the ski lift. Before 1939, skiers skied down to Government Camp and got rides back up to the lodge. The three-story building features 70 guest rooms, an 80-foot-tall chimney with six fireplaces, and a 700-pound weather vane. The lodge is famous for appearing in Stanley Kubrick's 1980 film *The Shining*.

Lige Coalman built this cabin in 1916 at Camp Blossom near the future site of Timberline Lodge. The area was popular with climbers and skiers, many of whom sought shelter in the cabin during bad weather. In the 1920s, the Mazamas nailed yellow arrows to nearby trees to guide climbers who had reached the mountain's timberline but did not know where they were.

For the hardy and willing, a winter trek up to the Camp Blossom area could be rewarding. At 2,000 feet above Government Camp, skiers and snowshoers were on their own, with only the refuge of the primitive Timberline Cabin if the weather turned bad. From 1924 to 1930, the Timberline Hotel (a collection of three tents) operated here.

Before construction could begin on Timberline Lodge in the spring of 1936, crews first had to remove the snow from the access road. Road-clearing started in March and was expected to take four weeks, but it took three months. Spring snowfall often replaced the snow that had been removed, with overall snow depth measuring 47 inches on March 5 and 90 inches by the end of March.

This 1936 photograph shows workers excavating land in preparation for construction of the east wing of Timberline Lodge. Despite the short construction season on the mountain, workers managed to completely frame the building between mid-June and October. Interior work was completed over the course of 1937, and the lodge opened in February 1938.

In March 1936, the former Civilian Conservation Corps camp at Summit Meadows was converted into a Works Progress Administration camp for the workers building Timberline Lodge. Snow had to be cleared and the abandoned camp had to be refurbished before the men could move in. The camp had a machine shop, a sawmill, a mess hall, and a cookhouse. Eight-man canvas

tents on four-foot-high wooden platforms were each warmed with a potbellied stove. During the winter of 1936–1937, the camp received seven feet of snow. The workers ate well, with breakfasts of fried ham, eggs, and sausage; lunches of sandwiches, soup, and apples; and dinners of steak, fish, potatoes, beans, and corn. During the peak of construction, up to 470 men stayed at the camp.

This photograph shows Timberline Lodge in the summer of 1937, when workers were busy installing furniture, light fixtures, and artwork. The project was so rushed that many details for the lodge's interior were not figured out until construction had started. Workers scrambled to do as much as they could before Pres. Franklin D. Roosevelt arrived in September to dedicate the lodge.

Pres. Franklin D. Roosevelt scheduled a trip to Oregon in 1937 to dedicate both the Bonneville Dam and Timberline Lodge. On September 28, his motorcade drove up to the lodge, where he took the elevator to the main floor. He made a speech from the terrace, with its crystal-clear view south to Mount Jefferson. Five hours later, with Roosevelt long gone, a blizzard descended on the mountain. (George M. Henderson.)

This undated aerial photograph shows the swimming pool at the end of the west wing. When Timberline Lodge opened, it did not have a pool. A pool was in the plans, but it was nixed by regional forester C.J. Buck in 1938 as being "a distinct step away from mountain recreation activities." The pool was finally built in 1958 and was advertised as the highest pool in the Northwest.

When Timberline Lodge opened to the public in 1938, the planned toboggan runs, ski jump, and skating rink were nonexistent due to lack of funds. However, the lodge attracted downhill skiers from the very beginning, even before construction of the first chairlift. Today, it is the only place in the United States with year-round lift-served skiing.

Timberline Lodge celebrated its first New Year's Eve with two orchestras and zero vacancies. A special guest for the evening was Emerson J. Griffith, director of Oregon's Works Progress Administration. Griffith was responsible for submitting the application to build the lodge, which outlined plans for roads, parking, trails, ski runs, a swimming pool, tennis courts, an amphitheater, barns, shelters, and—of course—the hotel itself.

Horseback riding among summer recreational opportunities at Timberline Lodge. The lodge kept horses that were used for guided horseback tours along the trails and bridle paths of Mount Hood. Col. Hartwell W. Palmer, a retired World War I cavalry officer, led horse tours along trails near Timberline Lodge from 1938 to 1942. The lodge stopped offering horse tours in the 1950s.

Snowcats have been in use on Mount Hood since 1937, when the first one was designed for hauling rock to the Timberline Lodge construction site. This snowcat was transporting skiers up the mountain from the lodge.

Saint Bernard dogs have served as the mascots of Timberline Lodge since it opened in 1937. Pictured here are the first dogs, Lady and Bruel. Since the 1960s, the popular 200-pound mascots have always been named Heidi and Bruno. The dogs are trained to greet and interact with up to 2,000 visitors a day.

15-654 Main Dining Room - Timberline Lodge - Mt. Hood, Oregon

15-596 Writing Nook - Lobby, Timberline Lodge - Oregon

The Cascade Dining Room in the east wing can seat more than 100 diners at a time. The handcrafted tables and chairs are made of Douglas fir from Oregon forests. The 14 light fixtures on the ceiling are painted burnt red and yellow ochre and resemble Native American drums. Eric Lamade's relief carving above the fireplace depicts bear, deer, and beaver and is called *Forest Scene*. (Cheryl Hill.)

This photograph shows a writing nook with the type of handcrafted furniture found throughout Timberline Lodge. One of the lodge's signature wrought-iron light fixtures is also visible here. Works Progress Administration blacksmiths created all the pieces by hand using smithing techniques that pioneers would have used. Funds for the lodge's furniture and artwork mostly came from the Federal Art Project, which ran from 1935 to 1943. (Cheryl Hill.)

The Ski Lounge on the lower level had rawhide-and-iron chairs for visitors to sit on. During the first winter that Timberline Lodge was open, it did a brisk business. But when ski season ended, the number of visitors dropped off, and many of those who did come were not staying overnight or eating in the restaurants. A 25¢ fee was imposed on anyone who wanted to visit any floors above the Ski Lounge, but the fee was abolished in 1940. The ski lounge was converted into the Lower Lobby in 1986 after the Wy'East Day Lodge for skiers was built. (Cheryl Hill.)

The main lounge is two stories tall and contains handmade couches and coffee tables that are clustered around a central stone chimney. The flooring is made of one-inch-thick oak planks. The six large wooden columns that support the soaring ceiling were hand-hewn by famed local cabin builder Henry Steiner. (Cheryl Hill.)

Named after Ferdinand A. Silcox, chief forester from 1933 to 1939, Silcox Hut was built on the south side of Mount Hood in 1939. Situated at 6,950 feet, it is 1,000 feet higher than Timberline Lodge. It was built to serve as a warming hut and to house the upper terminal of the Magic Mile chairlift. Many of the craftsmen who worked on Timberline Lodge also worked on the hut.

The Magic Mile chairlift was the second chairlift built in the United States and the first to use steel towers. When ski season ended, sunset lift rides were offered in the summer. In 1962, the Magic Mile chairlift was moved, and Silcox Hut was abandoned. It was severely vandalized but was eventually restored and reopened in 1993. It is now rented out for weddings and other events.

BIBLIOGRAPHY

Anderson, Rolf, ed. *We Had an Objective in Mind: The U.S. Forest Service in the Pacific Northwest 1905 to 2005*. Portland, OR: Pacific Northwest USFS Association, 2005.

Bell, Jon. *On Mount Hood: A Biography of Oregon's Perilous Peak*. Seattle, WA: Sasquatch Books, 2010.

Clackamas County Historical Society and Wasco County Historical Society. *Barlow Road*. Oregon City, OR: Clackamas County Historical Society, 1991.

Everest, F. Alton. *Tales of High Clackamas Country: An Anecdotal History of Experiences on the Lakes Ranger District of the Mount Hood National Forest, 1930–1935*. Sandy, OR: St. Paul's Press, 1993.

Grauer, Jack. *Mount Hood: A Complete History*. Vancouver, WA: Jack Grauer Publisher, 2010.

Henderson, George M. *Lonely on the Mountain: A Skier's Memoir*. Victoria, BC: Trafford Publishing, 2006.

Lewis, James G. *The USFS and the Greatest Good: A Centennial History*. Durham, NC: The Forest History Society, 2005.

Lowe, Don and Roberta. *Mount Hood: Portrait of a Magnificent Mountain*. Caldwell, ID: The Caxton Printers, Ltd, 1975.

McArthur, Lewis A. *Oregon Geographic Names*. Portland, OR: Oregon Historical Society Press, 2003.

McNeil, Fred H. *McNeil's Mount Hood*. Zigzag, OR: The Zig Zag Papers, 1990.

Munro, Sarah Baker. *Timberline Lodge: The History, Art, and Craft of an American Icon*. Portland, OR: Timber Press, 2009.

Oregon Writers' Program. *Mount Hood: A Guide*. New York: Duell, Sloan and Pearce, 1940.

Short, Casey. *Water: Portland's Precious Heritage*. Portland, OR: City of Portland, 2011.

Williams, Gerald W. *The U.S. Forest Service in the Pacific Northwest: A History*. Corvallis, OR: Oregon State University Press, 2009.

DISCOVER THOUSANDS OF LOCAL HISTORY BOOKS
FEATURING MILLIONS OF VINTAGE IMAGES

Arcadia Publishing, the leading local history publisher in the United States, is committed to making history accessible and meaningful through publishing books that celebrate and preserve the heritage of America's people and places.

Find more books like this at
www.arcadiapublishing.com

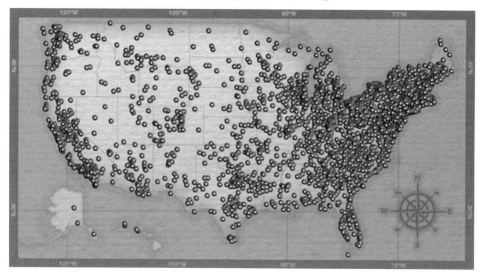

Search for your hometown history, your old stomping grounds, and even your favorite sports team.